GREAT
AMERICAN PRESIDENTS

THEODORE
ROOSEVELT

GREAT
AMERICAN PRESIDENTS

JOHN ADAMS

JOHN QUINCY ADAMS

JIMMY CARTER

THOMAS JEFFERSON

JOHN F. KENNEDY

ABRAHAM LINCOLN

RONALD REAGAN

FRANKLIN DELANO ROOSEVELT

THEODORE ROOSEVELT

HARRY S. TRUMAN

GEORGE WASHINGTON

WOODROW WILSON

GREAT
AMERICAN PRESIDENTS

THEODORE
ROOSEVELT

ALISON TURNBULL KELLEY

FOREWORD BY
WALTER CRONKITE

CHELSEA HOUSE
PUBLISHERS
A Haights Cross Communications Company

Philadelphia

CHELSEA HOUSE PUBLISHERS

VP, NEW PRODUCT DEVELOPMENT Sally Cheney
DIRECTOR OF PRODUCTION Kim Shinners
CREATIVE MANAGER Takeshi Takahashi
MANUFACTURING MANAGER Diann Grasse

STAFF FOR THEODORE ROOSEVELT

ASSISTANT EDITOR Kate Sullivan
PRODUCTION ASSISTANT Megan Emery
PHOTO EDITOR Sarah Bloom
SERIES DESIGNER Keith Trego
COVER DESIGNER Keith Trego
LAYOUT 21st Century Publishing and Communications, Inc.

A Haights Cross Communications ✦ Company

www.chelseahouse.com

First Printing

1 3 5 7 9 8 6 4 2

Library of Congress Cataloging-in-Publication Data

Kelley, Alison.
    Theodore Roosevelt / by Alison Turnbull Kelley.
        p. cm.—(Great American presidents)
Summary: A biography of the New Yorker who became governor of his state, vice president
under McKinley, and twenty-sixth president of the United States. Includes bibliographical
references and index.
    ISBN 0-7910-7606-7 (Hardcover)
    1. Roosevelt, Theodore, 1858-1919—Juvenile literature. 2. Presidents—United States—
Biography—Juvenile literature. [1. Roosevelt, Theodore, 1858-1919. 2. Presidents.]
I. Title. II. Series.
E757.K28 2003
973.91'1'092—dc21
                                                                                    2003009496

TABLE OF CONTENTS

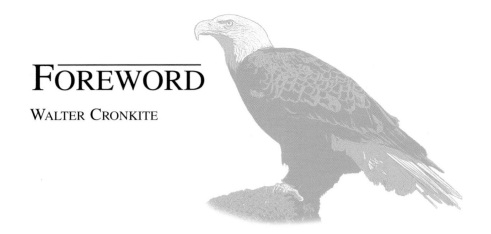

FOREWORD

WALTER CRONKITE

A candle can defy the darkness. It need not have the power of a great searchlight to be a welcome break from the gloom of night. So it goes in the assessment of leadership. He who lights the candle may not have the skill or imagination to turn the light that flickers for a moment into a perpetual glow, but history will assign credit to the degree it is due.

Some of our great American presidents may have had a single moment that bridged the chasm between the ordinary and the exceptional. Others may have assured their lofty place in our history through the sum total of their accomplishments.

When asked who were our greatest presidents, we cannot fail to open our list with the Founding Fathers who put together this nation and nursed it through the difficult years of its infancy. George Washington, John Adams, Thomas Jefferson, and James Madison took the high principles of the revolution against British tyranny and turned the concept of democracy into a nation that became the beacon of hope to oppressed peoples around the globe.

Almost invariably we add to that list our wartime presidents—Abraham Lincoln, perhaps Woodrow Wilson, and certainly Franklin Delano Roosevelt.

Nonetheless there is a thread of irony that runs through the inclusion of the names of those wartime presidents: In many aspects their leadership was enhanced by the fact that, without objection from the people, they assumed extraordinary powers to pursue victory over the nation's enemies (or, in the case of Lincoln, the Southern states).

The complexities of the democratic procedures by which the United States Constitution deliberately tried to withhold unchecked power from the presidency encumbered the presidents who needed their hands freed of the entangling bureaucracy that is the federal government.

Much of our history is written far after the events themselves took place. History may be amended by a much later generation seeking a precedent to justify an action considered necessary at the latter time. The history, in a sense, becomes what later generations interpret it to be.

President Jefferson in 1803 negotiated the purchase of vast lands in the south and west of North America from the French. The deal became knows as the Louisiana Purchase. A century and a half later, to justify seizing the nation's steel mills that were being shut down by a labor strike, President Truman cited the Louisiana Purchase as a case when the president in a major matter ignored Congress and acted almost solely on his own authority.

The case went to the Supreme Court, which overturned Truman six to three. The chief justice, Fred Vinson, was one of the three justices who supported the president. Many historians, however, agreed with the court's majority, pointing out that Jefferson scarcely acted alone: Members of Congress were in the forefront of the agitation to consummate the Louisiana Purchase and Congress voted to fund it.

With more than two centuries of history and precedent now behind us, the Constitution is still found to be flexible when honest and sincere individuals support their own causes with quite different readings of it. These are the questions that end up for interpretation by the Supreme Court.

As late as the early years of the twenty-first century, perhaps the most fateful decision any president ever can make—to commit the nation to war—was again debated and precedent ignored. The Constitution says that only the Congress has the authority to declare war. Yet the Congress, with the objection of few members, ignored this Constitutional provision and voted to give President George W. Bush the right to take the United States to war whenever and under whatever conditions he decided.

Thus a president's place in history may well be determined by how much power he seizes or is granted in re-interpreting and circumventing the remarkable document that is the Constitution. Although the Founding Fathers thought they had spelled out the president's authority in their clear division of powers between the branches of the executive, the legislative and the judiciary, their wisdom has been challenged frequently by ensuing generations. The need and the demand for change is dictated by the march of events, the vast alterations in society, the global condition beyond our influence, and the progress of technology far beyond the imaginations of any of the generations which preceded them.

The extent to which the powers of the presidency will be enhanced and utilized by the chief executives to come in large degree will depend, as they have throughout our history, on the character of the presidents themselves. The limitations on those powers, in turn, will depend on the strength and will of those other two legs of the three-legged stool of American government—the legislative and the judiciary.

And as long as this nation remains a democracy, the final say will rest with an educated electorate in perpetual exercise of its constitutional rights to free speech and a free and alert press.

1

A PRIVILEGED YOUTH

BUFFALO BILL CALLED him a "cyclone." Mark Twain called him an "earthquake, a buzz saw." However, this dynamic man, the 26th president of the United States, didn't start out all fire and energy.

Theodore Roosevelt started out as a frail, sickly boy who spent much of his childhood in bed reading books about nature. Growing up, he wanted to be a naturalist (a person who studies natural history), but as he got older, his calling changed.

He emerged from Harvard a strong, healthy, politically minded young man and was soon elected to the New York

Theodore Roosevelt, pictured here at age four, was known as "Teedie" in his youth. As a child, Theodore was often ill, suffering from asthma attacks that kept him from playing in the Roosevelt family's spirited games.

State legislature, where he would plant the seeds of a political life that would blossom into the United States presidency.

Despite the many twists and turns of his life, one thing remained constant: Theodore Roosevelt never lost his interest in natural history or his concern for protecting the environment.

THEODORE'S FAMILY

Born October 27, 1858, a strapping 8½ pounds, Theodore—called Teedie in his early years—was the second child of Theodore Roosevelt Sr. and Martha Bulloch Roosevelt. He had an older sister, Anna (affectionately called Bamie); a younger sister, Corinne; and a younger brother, Elliott. The Roosevelt family lived in wealth and comfort on a fashionable street in New York City.

Theodore's father was a powerfully built man with a full beard. His Dutch ancestors came to America from Holland in the seventeenth century. They were hardworking people who amassed a fortune from the family business of glass importing and later from real estate. Theodore Sr. was intelligent, conservative, and devoted to his family. Unlike many wealthy people, he believed that he had a duty to help people who were less fortunate. His mother, Margaret Barnhill Roosevelt, was an English-Irish Quaker who instilled in her children the principle of *noblesse oblige*—that wealth imposes social obligations. This spirit inflamed Theodore Sr., and he passed it on to his children.

Theodore Sr. devoted much of his time to charities and was beloved for his good works. He helped create the Children's Aid Society, a fund that helped the 20,000 homeless children in New York City. This organization laid the foundation for the Newsboys' Lodging House, where a boy could sleep in a bed for five cents a night. Theodore Sr. also helped to found the New York Orthopedic Hospital, which treated children with spinal deformities. Because his daughter Bamie had a painful and deforming spinal condition, he had a special interest in helping children with spinal problems.

Once a week, Theodore Sr. walked to the Lodging House and talked to the boys who stayed there. Theodore Jr. and Elliott sometimes accompanied him. In addition

PRESIDENT ROOSEVELT'S LEGACY

A Tradition of Public Service

Theodore Roosevelt Sr. instilled in his children a sense of responsibility to help people less fortunate and to treat all people fairly. His son Teddy proclaimed these values in his Square Deal platform, which promoted fair business competition and increased welfare for the needy.

Franklin Delano Roosevelt, fifth cousin of Theodore and a great admirer of him, carried on an ideal of fairness to the American people. As 32nd president (1933–1945), he promoted a New Deal, which involved measures for preventing banks from collapsing, emergency conservation and soil conservation projects, and additional relief funds for the needy.

In the mid-1900s, the head of another wealthy family, Joseph Kennedy Sr., also instilled a tradition of dedication to public service, a determination to succeed, and loyalty to his family. From this political family came the 35th U.S. president, John F. Kennedy, whose platform was the idealistic New Frontier. Kennedy supported equal rights and opportunities for citizens of all races. By creating the Peace Corps in 1961, he extended human service to countries in the developing world.

to showing that he cared for people who had to struggle to live, Theodore Sr. instilled a sense of responsibility in his children.

Theodore Sr. was a wonderful father and had great interest in and compassion for his children. The four Roosevelt children adored him. Theodore Jr. could think of nothing worse than disappointing his beloved father. As an adult, he wrote:

> My father . . . was the best man I ever knew. He combined strength and courage with gentleness, tenderness, and great unselfishness. He would not tolerate in us children selfishness or cruelty, idleness, cowardice, or untruthfulness.

Theodore Jr.'s mother was called Mittie. She was small, fragile, and beautiful, with dark hair and blue eyes. She had a wonderful sense of humor and was a great storyteller. Mittie spent many hours entertaining her children with stories of life on the Virginia plantation where she was born. She also told stories about legendary heroes such as Daniel Boone and Davy Crockett and about the real heroes in her own family during the Civil War (1861–1865).

Mittie's brothers were true Confederate war heroes. Her brother James was an admiral in the Confederate navy. He masterminded the secret building of the ship *Alabama*, among others. The *Alabama* went on to sink or capture 57 Union ships. Mittie's brother Daniel joined the Georgia Volunteers. Her youngest brother, Irvine, served on the *Alabama* and is believed to have fired the last shot before the ship went down in a battle with the *Kearsage* in 1864 (he was rescued). All of the men in Mittie's family and extended family served on the side of the South during the war.

Theodore Sr. did not serve in the Union army out of respect for Mittie's family and their support of the Confederacy. He paid a substitute to take his place, which was legal but also very expensive. Instead of fighting, Theodore Sr. participated in volunteer activities to help the Union soldiers at home during the war. Theodore Jr. never understood why his father didn't join in the actual fighting.

POOR HEALTH

Young Theodore caught many colds and had many stomachaches. At age three, he had his first attack of asthma, a condition marked by sudden recurring attacks of labored breathing, wheezing, gasping, and coughing. These attacks lasted hours or even days, with Theodore struggling to catch his breath. His lungs were weak, and he spent many nights propped up in bed on pillows. His father walked with him for hours to help him get his breath. He even took Theodore out at night for fast rides in a horse and carriage, hoping to force air into his son's weak lungs. Because of his early sickness, Theodore was educated mainly by private tutors until he went to college.

Sickly and small, Theodore often couldn't join in his family's spirited games. He instead spent time alone reading and writing adventures and tales of heroism. Theodore loved to hear and read tales of adventure, especially those that took place on the frontier. He read the books of Captain Mayne Reid, whose stories of adventure, action, and violence were peppered with abundant descriptions of plants and animals. Theodore also devoured books about natural history and had a special interest in birds. Throughout his life, Theodore Roosevelt never lost his love of reading.

THE ROOSEVELT MUSEUM
OF NATURAL HISTORY

One day while walking in New York City, seven-year-old Theodore saw a dead seal laid out on a piece of wood in front of a neighborhood market. Fascinated and curious, he kept going back to look at the seal, measuring it with a ruler and writing down information about it. He wanted to know everything about that seal—all of its measurements, how it died, where it came from, and how it got there. He begged the shop owner to sell him the seal. The shop owner refused, but he did give Theodore the seal's skull—a real prize to the young boy. To honor this special acquisition, Theodore and his cousins created the

> *"While my interest in natural history has added very little to my sum of achievement, it has added immeasurably to my sum of enjoyment in life."*
> —Theodore Roosevelt

Roosevelt Museum of Natural History in his room. Later, when the Roosevelts moved to a house near Central Park in New York City, much of the attic became Theodore's museum. He charged a penny for admission, but children were admitted free if they helped with the specimens.

Theodore's interest in all things of nature resulted in many odd incidents in the Roosevelt household. He collected animal specimens such as frogs, snails, turtles, and mice—dead or alive. At one time, he fed a litter of baby squirrels with an eyedropper three times a day. He also tied snapping turtles to the laundry tub. Once he asked the cook to boil a dead woodchuck that he had found. The cook refused and made him throw it out.

Mittie Roosevelt indulged and encouraged her son's interests, but when Theodore stored dead mice in the family's icebox (an early refrigerator that held ice to cool foods), Mittie quickly threw them away. She felt she had to put some limits on what she would allow her son to do. Theodore disagreed with his mother's decision and called throwing the mice out a "loss to science."

To add to his specimen collection, young Theodore placed an advertisement in the newspaper saying that he would buy live field mice for 10 cents per mouse or 35 cents for a family of mice. Unfortunately, the ad appeared just after the family (except for Bamie) left to go to the Berkshires, a mountain resort area in

Massachusetts, for the summer. To Bamie's horror, people brought hundreds of field mice to the house while Theodore was away.

By the time Theodore was 10 years old, he was writing about the characteristics of many insects, which he learned by observation. He was making a serious study of nature.

EARLY TEEN YEARS

Theodore's parents believed that travel abroad would be a wonderful education for the children, so in 1869, they decided to take the family to Europe for one full year.

Theodore, Elliott, Bamie, and Corinne didn't want to go to Europe. They wanted to spend their summers bare-foot and to ride their horse, Pony Grant. The children learned much about different cultures, but they appreciated the European trip mostly in retrospect. Nevertheless, while in and out of 66 hotels and traveling on trains, stagecoaches, steamships, horses, and donkeys, the children made their own fun. They had pillow fights and towel fights, jumped on hotel beds, hid in closets, and teased the maids.

By 1870, 12-year-old Theodore's health had still not improved, and he looked frail. Theodore had many bouts of sickness while on the European trip, but he didn't write much about these in his journals because he was used to it. Theodore's father, however, worried that his son would never be well, so he told him, "Theodore,

When Theodore was 11 years old, his parents decided to take the family on an extended European vacation. Photographed in Paris in 1870, Theodore was still frail and sickly, and he soon determined to "make [his] body" by lifting weights and exercising to develop physical strength.

you have the mind but you have not the body, and without the help of the body the mind cannot go as far as it should. You must *make* your body."

"I'll make my body," said a determined Theodore.

Theodore Sr. converted a second floor porch of their home into a gymnasium for the children. Theodore worked hard lifting weights, pulling rings, and using the horizontal bars. Very slowly, Theodore grew stronger. He also learned how to box. It wasn't until he was in college, however, that he felt any real stamina.

> "Having been a sickly boy . . . I was at first unable to hold my own when thrown into contact with other boys of rougher antecedents. I was nervous and timid. Yet . . . I felt a great admiration for men who were fearless and who could hold their own in the world."
>
> —Theodore Roosevelt,
> *An Autobiography*, 1913

By the time he was 13, Theodore's observational skills had improved greatly, so his father arranged for him to learn taxidermy (the science of preserving animals by skinning, stuffing, and mounting them). At last he learned the correct way to collect and preserve the animal specimens that he so loved. Learning techniques of taxidermy was the first of three things that changed Theodore's life as a young teen.

At 14, Theodore received his first gun from his father. He discovered that he liked to hunt and shoot birds in the woods. He loved birds, but he enjoyed studying them, too. Owning specimens was a way of studying them and a way of owning a part of nature. Theodore's interest in hunting continued, and he pursued it all his life, even going on safaris and bringing back specimens that became parts of Smithsonian collections.

While Theodore was learning to use his gun, he realized that he couldn't see his targets very clearly. Although he was able to read, he could not see more than 30 feet in front of him. His father had his eyes tested, and sure enough, Theodore needed glasses. When Theodore put on his first pair of glasses, his perception of the world literally changed. "I had no idea how beautiful the world was until I got those spectacles," he later said.

BUDDING SCIENTIST

In 1872, when Theodore was 14, the Roosevelt family took another trip abroad to many countries, including Egypt. The family planned to live on a houseboat on the Nile River in Egypt for a while. Theodore dreamed of all the exotic birds he would see. The trip appealed to him because he saw an opportunity to use his skinning and stuffing skills and equipment. On this trip, he began to seriously collect bird specimens. He watched, made notes, and described the birds in scientific terms, using their Latin names. He shot birds and skinned, cleaned, and mounted the specimens, which totaled over one hundred. His siblings complained of the chemical smells, of Theodore's smell, and of the whole project, but it was worth his time: Many of Theodore's specimens were later donated to the Smithsonian Institute and can still be seen there.

Theodore kept up with his bodybuilding and read more voraciously than ever. He studied many subjects. Armed

By the time he was a teenager, Theodore (top left, with Corinne, Elliot, and future wife Edith Carow), had become stronger physically. He also developed mentally; at 18 years of age, Theodore was a promising naturalist and had been accepted to prestigious Harvard College in Cambridge, Massachusetts.

with a diary, essays, specimen collections, and a burning enthusiasm for natural history, Theodore, a budding scientist, was ready for a life and career as a naturalist. In 1876, he took college entrance examinations in eight subjects and passed them all. Always a good student, Theodore was accepted into Harvard College in Cambridge, Massachusetts, and began college life away from his home and family for the first time.

2

THE YOUNG REFORMER

NO LONGER SO puny but still far from healthy-looking, Theodore arrived at Harvard with great enthusiasm. The family had decided that because of his health he would not live on campus among the other boys. His sister Bamie found an apartment for him and had it furnished.

Theodore was very happy at Harvard, although it took him some time to settle in to the campus routine and to find friends. All teeth, with squinty eyes behind thick glasses, Theodore also had a squeaky voice, especially when he laughed or was excited—which was often. His excitement over what he was saying made his words tumble out with machine-gun rapidity,

Teddy, photographed as a freshman at Harvard College in 1876, was a dedicated and serious student. Unlike his peers, Teddy avoided the temptations of living away from home for the first time and spent his time studying or participating in extracurricular activities.

which startled his listeners. Some students poked fun at him, but his great enthusiasm and friendliness eventually earned him good friends.

Theodore was shocked to learn that many of his class-mates were at Harvard not to learn but to have a good time. Fun-loving as he was, Theodore was serious about his studies. His father wrote to him, "Take care of your morals first, your health next, and finally your studies." Theodore replied, "I do not find it nearly so hard as I expected not to drink and smoke . . . ."

Weekly letters passed back and forth between New York and Boston. One of the things Theodore wrote to his family was how much his asthma had improved. It was quite sudden and miraculous. He also began signing his letters with different names: Thee Jr., Theodore, Ted, Teddy, or Tedo. He couldn't decide what to call himself. "Teddy" is the name that stuck.

When Teddy arrived at Harvard as a freshman, he intended to study the sciences and become a naturalist. He showed other interests as well, joining the Hasty Pudding Club (the drama club, which still exists), the Art Club, the Finance Club, the Rifle Club, and the Glee (Chorus) Club. He also continued his physical workouts, though his progress was still slow.

In February 1878, during his sophomore year, Teddy got word that his father was seriously ill. He traveled back to New York, but Theodore Sr. died before he reached home. Teddy remembered his father lovingly in later years, saying, "He was the most wise and loving father that ever lived; I owe everything to him."

Teddy was devastated, but he returned to Harvard and continued his studies. His way of dealing with his grief was to plunge into studies, sports, magazine writing, clubs, and other activities. He also studied history and law and was very interested in writing. He combined two of those interests—naval stories and writing—in his last years at Harvard by beginning to write a book, *The Naval War of 1812.*

At some point during his college years, Teddy became interested in politics. He decided against science as a career and resolved to go to law school. By being a lawyer, he could fulfill his obligation as a person of wealth to help those less fortunate, as his father had taught him.

ALICE HATHAWAY LEE

During Teddy's third year at Harvard, he fell in love with Alice Hathaway Lee, a sweet, pretty 17-year-old. Alice was bright and lively. She also came from a wealthy family. Alice was not a student at Harvard; she was a neighbor of one of Teddy's classmates. The Lee family lived in a suburb of Boston—Chestnut Hill—that was about six miles from Harvard. Six miles was a bit far for courtship in the days before automobiles crowded the roads. Teddy had his horse, Lightfoot, shipped to him from New York so that he could make the ride to see Alice often and so that he did not have to depend on a friend from school to take him. Teddy was completely smitten with Alice and wrote long passages about her in his diary, writing her name over and over: *Alice, Alice, Alice.*

When Teddy was a senior, he asked Alice to marry him. At first she refused but later, she, too, fell in love. In

Alice Hathaway Lee was a pretty and energetic girl from a wealthy family. Roosevelt fell in love with Alice in his third year at Harvard; in 1880, she agreed to marry him and the newlyweds moved in with Teddy's mother in New York City while he attended Columbia Law School.

January 1880, Teddy and Alice became engaged. On February 13, Teddy wrote:

> I do not think ever a man loved a woman more than I love her; for a year and a quarter now I have *never* (even when hunting) gone to sleep or waked up without thinking of her; and I doubt if an hour has passed that I have not thought of her.

On October 27, 1880, in the fall after Teddy's graduation from Harvard, Alice and Teddy were married and began their life together. He was 21; she was 19. The couple lived with Mittie in the Roosevelt family home in New York City while Teddy went to law school at Columbia University. Meanwhile, he continued writing *The Naval War of 1812*.

He soon became restless and dissatisfied with the study of law, which he didn't think had enough to do with justice. He decided to work for the cause of justice by going into politics.

ENTERING POLITICS

In the society in which Teddy Roosevelt lived, people from wealthy, aristocratic families like the Roosevelts did not directly participate in politics. That was for the governing class. "Gentlemen" worked on the sidelines, supported good causes, and didn't mix with politicians. Teddy didn't care about following those rules. He started out by stopping in at a seedy-looking Republican headquarters located above a saloon, and he talked to the local politicians. At first they didn't know what to make of this aristocratic man in formal dress with gloves and cane, but they soon got to know and respect him.

"The first duty of an American citizen, then, is that he shall work in politics; his second duty is that he shall do that work in a practical manner; and his third is that it shall be done in accord with the highest principles of honor and justice."

—Theodore Roosevelt,
"The Duties of American Citizenship"
speech, January 26, 1883

After his first year of law school, Teddy and Alice took a delayed honeymoon abroad. Always looking for adventure, Teddy took time out to climb the Matterhorn, a challenging mountain almost 15,000 feet high that is part of the Alps mountain chain between Switzerland and Italy.

When the couple returned to New York, Teddy went back to law school and finished *The Naval War of 1812*. He again began dropping in on the local Republicans. This time they were happy to see him. He attended Republican meetings and expressed his disapproval of big bosses (of businesses) and corrupt political machines—groups of people with special interests.

It was at this time that people began to notice him. In fact, the Republican Party nominated him for state assembly in 1881. He ran for the office and was surprised to win the election by a landslide. Teddy began his political career at age 23—the youngest assemblyman in New York State.

Law school was out of the picture because of Teddy's position in the legislature; he would have to work in Albany, the capital of New York. He was content to leave law school, though, because he believed he was in the political arena, where he could accomplish needed changes.

When young Teddy first appeared in the assembly, he was not well received. His high-society dress and accent immediately set him apart. He said, "Mistah Speakah" when he addressed the assembly, and the other assemblymen mockingly called him "Young Squirt Lordship" or the "Exquisite Mr. Roosevelt." One assemblyman made a gravely insulting remark to Teddy in a tavern. After Teddy knocked the man down not once but three times, that kind of thing never happened again. Teddy's friendly and enthusiastic manner, however, eventually won him many friends within the assembly.

Teddy ultimately earned respect on the floor of the assembly. He had become quite an orator and had many causes for which he proposed legislation, all leading to abolishing corruption—particularly corrupt political practices—and focusing on New York City. He was elected for two more terms and earned a new nickname, "the Young Reformer." Teddy's dedica-

> *"I am only an average man, but, by George, I work harder at it than the average man."*
> —Theodore Roosevelt

tion, not to mention his intensity and drive, was apparent. He always went about things wholeheartedly. A friend said of him, "He would go at a thing as if the world was coming to an end." Young but politically experienced, Teddy came to learn that "politics is a matter of give and take."

HUNTING BUFFALO

Teddy had a brief bout of asthma in the summer of 1883, between his second and third terms of office. His doctor told him to go to a health spa, so he and Alice reluctantly went to a spa with sulfur springs that was located in the Catskill Mountains. After he started to feel better, Teddy tired of rest and sulfur. In fact, he longed for an adventure. He left Alice at home, took his gun, and, with a guide, went buffalo hunting in the Dakota Territory. Out in the open air, he felt better immediately.

While searching for buffalo, Teddy and his young guide, Joe Ferris, endured days of soaking rain punctuated by scorching sun. The extreme weather conditions didn't extinguish Teddy's love of the wilderness. Upon waking up out in the open in soaked blankets with water all around them, Teddy said to Joe, "By Godfrey, but this is fun!" Eventually, Teddy shot and killed a buffalo. He felt pure excitement over this long-awaited victory.

Teddy was so thrilled with being in the "country" that he decided to invest in 400 head of cattle. He made a deal with a cowboy to manage the cattle, and after going back to Albany for his third term in the legislature, he returned to the Dakota Territory from time to time.

DOUBLE TRAGEDY

Things were going well for Teddy. He and Alice were thrilled when they learned that Alice was pregnant. On February 12, 1884, during his third term, Teddy received a telegram in Albany saying that Alice had given birth to a baby girl and that mother and baby were doing fine. An ecstatic Teddy prepared for the journey home but didn't leave immediately. A few hours later, a second telegram brought terrible news. Alice was seriously ill with Bright's disease, an inflammation of the kidneys, and Mittie was very ill with typhoid fever, a serious bacterial infection that causes severe diarrhea, fever, weakness, headache, and other symptoms.

Teddy got on the next train to New York City in a blinding fog. When he reached Alice's bedside he held her and tried to soothe her, but she was barely conscious. After about four hours, someone came into the room and told Teddy that if he wanted to see his mother he'd better do it immediately. Mittie died with all four of her children around her. Alice lived 11 hours longer, with Teddy holding her the whole time. A double tragedy had hit on February 14, 1884—Valentine's Day. Teddy's brother Elliott declared, "There is a curse on this house."

Sick with grief but hiding his feelings, Teddy was a broken man when he returned to Albany to finish his term. He wrote, "When my heart's dearest died, the light went out from my life forever." After taking care of Alice's things, Teddy never said another word about Alice to their daughter, little Alice, or to anyone else as far as anyone knows.

ESCAPE TO DAKOTA

In 1884, Teddy suffered a political loss as well as personal losses. He was elected as delegate-at-large to the Republican National Convention in Chicago. He worked tirelessly for the candidate he supported, George F. Edmunds, who lost to James G. Blaine, a presidential candidate who had been accused of dishonesty in his business. To support the Republican Party, Teddy had to support Blaine. As a result, Teddy lost many friends and supporters. At this point,

Teddy left baby Alice with his sister Bamie, quit politics, and moved west to the Dakota Territory to become a cattle rancher. He used money that he inherited from his father to buy a ranch, which he called Elkhorn.

Teddy wrote to a friend, "Black care rarely sits behind a rider whose pace is fast enough." His grief was so deep and his despondency so encompassing that he tried to convince himself that he was leaving baby Alice for her own good. He said to his foreman and friend, Bill Sewall, "Her aunt can take care of her a good deal better than I can. She never would know anything about me, anyway. She would be just as well off without me." Teddy didn't really believe what he said. He wrote loving letters to Bamie, saying, "I miss both you and darling Baby Lee [Alice] dreadfully; kiss her many times for me; I am really hungry to see her." He also devoured Bamie's news about the baby.

When Teddy arrived in the Dakota Territory (now the states of North and South Dakota), he dressed himself in a cowboy outfit—broad sombrero, horsehide riding pants, fringed shirt with beads, alligator belt, and silver spurs. He also wore his glasses. He bought a pearl-handled gun and a Winchester rifle. Teddy Roosevelt was dressed for action.

The "real" cowboys snickered at Teddy's efforts to look like a cowboy. Behind his back they called him "Four Eyes" and "Storm Windows" because of his glasses, but Teddy knocked down a man who called him "Four Eyes" to his face. The local cowboys soon learned that Teddy was

After the deaths of his mother and wife, as well as political disappointments, Roosevelt escaped to the Elkhorn Ranch in the Dakota Territory. Although he was initially ridiculed by the "real" cowboys, Roosevelt eventually won their respect after he demonstrated his hunting and riding skills.

serious about being a cowboy and about his new venture as a cattle rancher. He bought 2,500 more head of cattle and hired a foreman to manage Elkhorn. He even decided to build a beautiful house on the property.

Teddy rode the open range and worked hard, always observing the wondrous scenes, birds, and animals of the prairie. He wrote, "It was a land of vast silent spaces, of lonely rivers, and of plains where the wild game stared at the passing horseman."

He worked hard alongside the cowboys, especially at the biannual roundups. During a roundup, cowboys located the thousands of cattle that had multiplied from the earlier seasons and separated them according to their brands. At this time, the many new calves that were born had to be branded. Teddy held his own in roundups, although he wasn't as skilled in roping as the experienced cowboys.

Teddy also participated in bronco busting—riding a horse that hasn't been saddled before—and showed great grit and staying power. "He's sure a man to hold up his end," one cowboy said. Teddy admired the cowboys he worked with, calling them "as hard and self-reliant as any men who ever breathed." There are many who would have said the same of Teddy Roosevelt.

Teddy frequently left the ranch to go on hunting expeditions, shooting doves, geese, and ducks; prairie chickens; elk, bighorn sheep; and antelope. He even shot a nine-foot, one-ton grizzly bear, whose skin he had made into a rug. He wrote about these hunting trips in books such as *Hunting Trips of a Rancher.*

Meanwhile, back east, Bamie was taking care of baby Alice and supervising the construction of Teddy's new huge home, called Sagamore Hill, at Oyster Bay, on Long Island, New York. Its walls, like those at his ranch, were decorated with the heads of animals that he had shot.

SEEDS OF CONSERVATION

Teddy observed that the buffalo and other large animals were disappearing because "man the destroyer" was over-hunting them, and he noticed the extreme dryness in the forests, which could easily lead to uncontrollable fires. He thought about ways to prevent certain environmental problems such as irrigation, topsoil runoff and ensuing flooding, and loss of game animals, which worried him. He believed very strongly that the United States needed a policy on conservation. Such a thing was unheard of in the country in the late 1800s.

> *"Every lover of nature who appreciates the majesty and beauty of the wilderness should strike hands with the far-sighted who wish to preserve our forests."*
> —Theodore Roosevelt, "Call for Conservationism," 1903

3

POLITICAL AND PERSONAL RENEWAL

TEDDY LEFT THE ranch to witness the completion of Sagamore Hill in the summer of 1885. He returned to Elkhorn Ranch in August but was back in New York by October 1885. While visiting his sister and baby Alice, he ran into 24-year-old Edith Carow, a childhood friend of the family and Teddy's former sweetheart. He didn't want to see Edith, perhaps because he knew he liked her very much and didn't want to be unfaithful to the memory of his beloved dead wife.

Teddy had serious misgivings about second marriages. He wrote to Bamie, "I utterly disbelieve in and disapprove of second marriages. I have always considered that they argued weakness in

Edith Carow was a childhood friend of Roosevelt's. Although he was hesitant to remarry out of respect for his deceased wife, Roosevelt secretly became engaged to Carow by November 1885, and they were married on December 2, 1886.

a man's character." Perhaps promises and declarations that he had made to Alice were plaguing him. Nevertheless, he rekindled his friendship with Edith, and they fell in love.

Edith was attractive, intellectual, cultured, gracious, disciplined, and strong-willed. She also came from a wealthy New York family. By November 17, 1885, Edith and Teddy were secretly engaged. It would be considered improper for Teddy to be courting a new woman when his wife had not been dead for two years. He and Edith decided to wait a year before marrying, so they made a plan to meet and marry privately in London. Meanwhile, Edith went on an extended trip to Europe with her mother and sister, and Teddy went back and forth from Sagamore Hill in New York to Elkhorn in Dakota.

In 1886, toward the end of the year of the couple's waiting, Teddy went to New York and attended the Republican convention for the county. The Labor Party was backing a solid candidate for mayor, but the Republicans did not have a particular candidate. At the convention, someone noticed Teddy in the crowd. A few days later, a Republican committee asked Teddy to run for mayor. Teddy was surprised, but he accepted.

Teddy Roosevelt approached the campaign with his usual vigor. He worked 18-hour days, giving three to five speeches per night. He loved it.

> "I always believe in going hard at everything."
> —Theodore Roosevelt in a letter to his son, Ted, May 7, 1901

Despite his enthusiastic campaigning, the Democratic candidate Abram Hewitt won. Teddy took it hard, but he had something to look forward to. He soon set sail for London to marry Edith.

On December 2, 1886, Teddy Roosevelt and Edith Carow were married in a private ceremony in London. The day was so thick with fog that even inside the church,

Teddy and Edith could barely see each other. The marriage was a surprise to everyone but Bamie, who knew about it from the beginning.

Teddy and Edith honeymooned in Europe and then returned to the United States to live at the now-completed Sagamore Hill in Oyster Bay. Alice, now three years old, moved in with them. Teddy and Edith showered little Alice with love and attention and soon began to have children of their own.

Teddy had overspent in building Sagamore Hill and in building his cattle business, so he decided to leave politics for a while. He would earn money writing and running his cattle ranch. The ranch wasn't doing well, however: Cattle were starving and might not live through a cold winter.

BOONE AND CROCKETT CLUB

The fiercely cold 1886–1887 Dakota winter killed many of the cattle. Those that survived were like walking skeletons. Teddy and Edith decided to sell the ranch, even though it meant losing more than half of Teddy's original investment. They also sold part of the land at Sagamore Hill and set out to economize. Teddy went back to writing to bring in some income. He began *The Winning of the West,* a four-volume history of the West and also wrote *Hunting Trips of a Ranchman* and *The Wilderness Hunter.*

Teddy enjoyed writing, but he missed politics. He saw many things about America that needed improving, and he wanted to be the instrument of improvement.

In 1887, Teddy came back from one of his regular

visits to Dakota country angry and frustrated. The wilderness was in danger from "swinish game-butchers," who were over-hunting and killing wild animals. Beavers were disappearing, and much of the land was drying up. Teddy was just one hunter, so he didn't consider his own game kills damaging to the balance of wildlife. Many travelers from the East, however, were killing buffalo for sport. American Indians were killing herds of buffalo for their tongues and to sell them to supply the popular demand. Another destructive practice was the "hounding of deer," in which hunters drove deer into the water for easy killing. What's more, precious trees were rapidly disappearing.

People acted as if all the treasures of nature were an endless supply. Teddy realized, as people of the later twentieth century also learned, that nature's wild areas and wildlife do not last forever. They must be preserved and nurtured. Such damage to animal life and the natural environment bothered Teddy terribly, and he wanted to do something about it.

Spurred on by these environmental concerns, Teddy and naturalist George Bird Grinnell formed the Boone and Crockett Club in 1887. The purpose of the club was to preserve the American wilderness. Other protective measures enacted by the federal government followed. In 1891, Congress passed the Forest Reserve Act. This gave the U.S. president the right to designate forestland to be protected in any state or territory, and it became the basis of our national forest system. In 1894, the Park Protection

Although Teddy was fond of hunting himself, he felt he did so responsibly. After returning from the Dakota Territory, Teddy became angry with the way in which other hunters were killing animals for profit and upsetting the balance of wildlife. He started the Boone and Crockett Club with another conservationist, George Bird Grinnell, to protect the environment.

Act, which protects Yellowstone National Park from "further destruction," was passed.

CIVIL SERVICE

Teddy's chance to re-enter politics came in 1889. President Benjamin Harrison offered Teddy the position of U.S. civil service commissioner in Washington, D.C. Teddy's friends thought that this job was not important enough for him, but Teddy saw it as an opportunity to go after corruption. He set to work reforming the "spoils system," which was rampant in New York politics. The spoils system was the custom of giving government positions to friends or political and financial supporters even if they were not qualified for the position.

Teddy went at it with his typical gusto. President Harrison remarked that Teddy "wanted to put an end to all the evil in the world between sunrise and sunset." When Teddy resigned from the civil service in 1895, he had gained admiration for attacking the injustices of the system.

Meanwhile, Teddy and Edith continued to add to their family. By 1895, at age 37, Teddy had four children in addition to Alice: Ted Jr. (eight), Kermit (six), Ethel (four), and Archibald (one), who was called Archie. Two years later, Teddy and Edith's last child, Quentin, was born.

The children played together, but the most raucous playmate of all was their father. Down on all fours, Teddy was a child playing among smaller children. Hide-and-seek was always a favorite game of his. He made up fun, exciting, and physical games and was the leader. Teddy's boyish enthusiasm endeared him to his children and to grownups as well.

This lively spirit propelled him in all his activities and interests. Perhaps he could apply the same

> *"For unflagging interest and enjoyment, a household of children, if things go reasonably well, certainly makes all other forms of success and achievement lose their importance by comparison."*
> —Theodore Roosevelt, *An Autobiography*, 1913

spirit and vigor to cleaning up corruption in the New York City Police Department. The new mayor of New York City thought so and offered Teddy the opportunity to be one of New York City's three police commissioners.

POLICE SLEUTH

Being a New York City police commissioner was a perfect job for a determined man like Teddy Roosevelt. As police commissioner, he found that corruption was everywhere. Disguised in a long overcoat with his hat pulled down, Teddy prowled the New York City streets at night. He caught policemen who were napping, drinking, or just not doing their job.

Teddy uncovered bribes, political favors, and abuse. Outraged, he fired many police officers, including high-ranking ones. He had a ploy to publicize his reform tactics: When he was about to fire a high-ranking police officer, he yelled "hi-yi-yi," in true cowboy fashion, out his office window. This got the attention of two reporters he had befriended whose office was across the street. The alerted reporters wrote stories about these crime-busting activities, and Teddy wanted the attention of the people in these reforms.

45

As New York City police commissioner, Teddy was more active than this picture implies. Dressed in an overcoat to hide his identity, he became famous for prowling the streets and uncovering many forms of police corruption.

In Teddy's efforts at reform, he also tried to enforce a law that was already in effect but overlooked. He attempted to prevent the sale of liquor in New York on Sunday. Many applauded him and many hated him for it, but it certainly got him attention across the whole country.

Teddy also rewarded courageous and hard-working police officers. He encouraged all policemen to be physically fit. By the time he left the police department in 1897, the New York City Police Department was an honest, efficient, and respected organization.

After only one year as police commissioner, Teddy was asked to campaign for William McKinley, who was running for his second term as president. Roosevelt snapped up the opportunity. Not only did he love speaking to crowds and trying to be persuasive—he now had a big, booming voice—but he hoped to be rewarded with a position he *really* wanted: assistant secretary of the United States Navy.

McKinley won the presidential election in 1896, but he hesitated to reward Roosevelt with a post. McKinley was intent on peace, and he interpreted Roosevelt's intensity as a readiness to go to war. Still, he did give Roosevelt the post of assistant secretary of the U.S. Navy. Roosevelt was thrilled.

4

THE
ROUGH RIDERS

BY THE TIME Roosevelt took the position of assistant secretary of the U.S. Navy in 1897, he and Edith had six children: Alice (fourteen), Teddy, Jr. (ten), Kermit (eight), Ethel (six), Archie (three), and Quentin (infant).

Roosevelt's great interest in naval history had convinced him that America needed a strong navy. He arrived in Washington quiet but with plans. He wanted to set Cuba and the Philippines free from Spain. He also wanted the United States to annex the Hawaiian Islands.

He was quiet for two months, but he couldn't keep still for long. In a speech to the Naval War College, Roosevelt let loose.

When Teddy took the position of assistant secretary of the Navy in 1897, his family had finished growing. This portrait of the Roosevelt family (from left to right: Quentin, Teddy, Ted Jr., Archie, Alice, Kermit, Edith, and Ethel) was taken six years later in 1903.

His opinions flew out in a fiery patriotic speech in which he talked about being ready for war as a means of keeping peace. In fact, he said "war" 62 times in his speech. Readiness for war, Roosevelt believed, involved enlarging the navy; he wanted America to be a world power. Roosevelt's boss, Secretary of the Navy John D. Long, was not happy with this flamboyant speech. Long, however, went on vacation and wasn't a part of the events that occurred soon after.

TROUBLE BREWING IN THE PACIFIC

Naval Secretary Long's choice for commander in chief of the Asiatic Station in the Pacific was Commodore William Chandler. Roosevelt was horrified at the thought of such a mild man possibly attacking Manila, so he persuaded President McKinley to appoint Commodore George Dewey. Long was not pleased, but he gave in.

In 1897, Commodore Dewey sailed to Hong Kong to prevent the Spanish ships from leaving the Philippines. This move paid off in May 1898, when the Spanish fleet was cleanly destroyed with no fatalities and almost no injuries. The Spaniards were expelled from Manila Harbor within hours, and the Philippine Islands were freed from Spain.

Meanwhile, on January 12, 1898, a riot in Havana, Cuba, threatened the safety of American citizens there. Roosevelt wanted the United States to go to Cuba. Naval Secretary Long didn't take it seriously. He was impatient with Roosevelt's reaction to the riot, but on January 25, McKinley had the battleship *Maine* positioned in Havana Harbor in Cuba as a warning, not as an aggressive act. On February 15, the *Maine* blew up, killing 266 Americans.

Teddy reacted to the explosion by sending a cable to the U.S. Navy fleet in the Pacific to be ready for war. Secretary Long was not pleased with Roosevelt's action, but within two weeks Congress declared war on Spain. The Pacific fleet was ready because of Teddy Roosevelt's cable.

The cause of the explosion is still not clear, but

Roosevelt believed it was the "dirty treachery" of the Spaniards. Historians believe this is unlikely.

In March, President McKinley wanted to peacefully negotiate with the Spaniards. The Spaniards also seemed willing, but Roosevelt had pushed the American people to look for war. Also, at that time, the published cause of the explosion was determined as an "external device," further inflaming the American populace.

THE SPANISH-AMERICAN WAR

Swayed by public opinion, President McKinley asked Congress to declare war. On April 19, 1898, the United States declared war on Spain. Thus began the Spanish-American War. Teddy Roosevelt wholeheartedly supported this move, believing that Cuba should gain its independence from Spain. Then he did what some people thought was a foolish, if not unusual, thing.

Against everyone's advice, Roosevelt resigned from the navy and helped to form a volunteer cavalry (troops on horseback). When friends and acquaintances, especially those from the Plains, heard that he was forming a regiment, they wanted to join. Many others also applied: A total of 23,000 applications came from all over the country. Roosevelt chose 1,000 men for their riding ability, marksmanship, toughness, and athleticism, and he placed himself second in command as colonel. He took out life insurance and bought 12 pairs of glasses. Teddy Roosevelt was ready for war.

Roosevelt led the regiment and joined the ranks of

Teddy Roosevelt and the Rough Riders stand at the top of the hill that they captured in San Juan. Teddy organized this volunteer regiment; out of 23,000 applicants, he chose 1,000 men and made himself second in command.

those he had always admired in stories he read. Everyone at home acted as if Roosevelt were in command. Newspapers even called the regiment Roosevelt's Rough Riders. The regiment wore blue neckerchiefs, had a bald eagle as mascot, and even had a kind of theme song: "There'll Be a Hot Time in the Old Town Tonight." The Rough Riders loved Roosevelt, and they remained very close throughout their lives.

After a short wait, orders came for the regiment to go to Tampa so that they could ship out to Cuba. In the end, however, word came that only 560 of the 1,000 men could go and that only the officers could take their horses. This was quite a blow. All the men had trained to fight on horseback. Those who could go would have to be foot soldiers. After many delays, Roosevelt's regiment and other regiments sailed to Cuba in 31 ships. Roosevelt was ecstatic.

The ships carrying regular army soldiers were supposed to reach Cuban shores first. Roosevelt was afraid his volunteer regiment wouldn't arrive in time to be in the fighting, so he somehow maneuvered his ship to get to shore first.

On shore, Roosevelt refused to ride his horse when the other men had to march in the pouring rain. He led his horse on foot but mounted it in battle. The regiment waited again and then received orders to go into the hills to attack the Spaniards.

To get inland to where the Spaniards were situated, the regiment had to tramp through a thick, dark jungle of twisted branches and dense undergrowth. Though the jungle was filled with fierce and determined soldiers, the mosquitoes were truly in command. Roosevelt himself found the damp jungle confusing, and he could barely see.

Eventually, when reaching open land, Roosevelt spotted the cone-shaped hats of the Spaniards in a trench while bullets whizzed by. This was the first time he witnessed death in battle. As the wounded men hit the ground, giant land crabs and vultures formed the final line of attack on the fallen.

The Rough Riders successfully routed the Spaniards in their first encounter. Roosevelt led the men up San Juan Hill, wading through a creek that was bloody and filled with dead bodies. The men had to crawl to be hidden from the enemy's sight and passed right by the Army regulars who were waiting for orders to attack.

> "The good man should be both a strong and a brave man; that is he should be able to fight, he should be able to serve his country as a soldier, if the need arises."
> —Theodore Roosevelt, "Citizenship in a Republic" speech, April 23, 1910

When they advanced, the Rough Riders first took Kettle Hill. The besieged Spaniards ran from the Americans, leaving their food behind. The hungry Rough Riders cooked the food and ate it "with relish!" On Kettle Hill, the men set up camp, tended the wounded, and waited for their next orders. Roosevelt took the time to pick up three empty shells to take home to his boys as souvenirs. Always a great letter writer, as were all the Roosevelts, Teddy wrote the following to his daughter Ethel in the short pause between battles:

Darling Ethel:

. . . . Here there are lots of funny lizards that run about in the dusty roads very fast and then stand still with their heads up. Beautiful red cardinal birds and tanagers flit about in the woods, and the flowers are lovely. But you never saw such dust. Sometimes I lie on the ground outside and sometimes in the tent. I have a mosquito net because there are so many mosquitoes.

Near Santiago, May 20, 1898

A week later, on July 1, 1898, the Rough Riders fought in the famous battle of San Juan Hill. Roosevelt rode forward on his horse but miraculously was not hurt in the bloody battle. The Americans won. In all, Roosevelt's regiment lost 89 men.

On July 17, 1898, a little more than two weeks after the battle of San Juan Hill, the Spaniards officially surrendered—with a strange request. Could the Americans first fire *over* the buildings in Santiago? That way, the general in command could report that he surrendered under fire. The Americans did just that.

After the surrender, the American troops were delayed in being brought home from Cuba. Many of them contracted malaria and died. The regular army hesitated to complain for fear of hurting their careers, but Roosevelt finally made their position public by sending a letter signed by his men to the Associated Press, infuriating Secretary of War Russell A. Alger as well as President McKinley. Roosevelt wrote:

> . . . that this army should at once be taken out of the Island of Cuba . . . that the army is disabled by malarial fever to the extent that its efficiency is destroyed, and that it is in a condition to be practically entirely destroyed by an epidemic of

yellow fever which is sure to come in the near future. . . . This army must be moved at once or perish. . . . the persons responsible for preventing such a move will be responsible for the unnecessary loss of many thousands of lives.

Three days later, the army had orders to leave Cuba.

In only a few weeks, the Americans had given the Cubans their country back. "Oh, we had a bully fight," Roosevelt said, using one of his favorite words. Fighting for what he believed was a good cause had invigorated him.

Roosevelt was very patriotic and very adventurous and had always admired war heroes. He wanted to participate in fighting partially because his father had never joined his compatriots on the battlefields during the Civil War. Young Theodore could never understand or accept that his father didn't take the opportunity to become a war hero. (Theodore Sr. always regretted not having gone into battle.) Teddy wanted to do something that his children could be proud of. He said to his good friend Henry Cabot Lodge that his part in the Spanish-American War would serve "as an apology for my having existed . . . should the worst come to the worst I am quite content to go now and to leave my children at least an honorable name."

Roosevelt thought he should be awarded a Congressional Medal of Honor, the highest award that can be bestowed on an individual serving in the Armed Services of the United States, given for valor in action against an enemy force. He did not receive it in his lifetime.

The Spanish-American War created a widely accepted image of Teddy Roosevelt as a hero. The popularity he achieved through his service in the conflict enabled him to win the governorship of New York State.

GOVERNOR OF NEW YORK

Americans cheered and welcomed Roosevelt back into the country on August 15, 1898. Teddy Roosevelt was a war hero. Soon there was talk about him running for governor of New York.

On September 17, 1898, Roosevelt announced that he would run for governor if nominated. The Republican Party did nominate him, and his popularity and fame from the Spanish-American War made it easy for him to win the campaign. On November 8, 1898, 39-year-old Teddy Roosevelt was elected governor of New York. People called him the "boy governor." Of the win, he said in classic Roosevelt fashion, "That's bully."

It was no surprise that Theodore Roosevelt's political platform included ridding New York of political machines and corrupt business practices. In addition, Roosevelt began his work of conservation, which grew and continued on a global scale long after his death. He later said of his work as governor:

> All that later I strove for in the Nation in connection with conservation was foreshadowed by what I strove to obtain for New York State when I was Governor.

As governor, Roosevelt was again a reformer. He knew he had much work to do, and he enjoyed it. At the top of his list was the protection of New York forestland. He supported laws to prevent pollution from sawmill industries that dumped chemical waste into streams and rivers. He urged restraint in harvesting lumber from forests, because he knew from his experiences in the West that the forest is necessary to absorb rainwater. He wrote that "unrestrained greed means the ruin of the great woods."

He urged the shutdown of businesses that used bird feathers or animal skins for decorating hats and other clothing.

One influential source for Roosevelt's conservation policy was Gifford Pinchot, who worked for the state forestry department system. Pinchot believed that lumber companies should replant the trees that they were allotted to take.

The Boone and Crockett Club that Roosevelt and George Bird Grinnell had formed in 1887 was also an aid in conserving wildlife. Its aim was to protect large game animals from being over-hunted so that there would always be animals for hunting in the future. Roosevelt was not against hunting, and in fact, hunters were a great part of the conservation movement in the 1880s. One

> "The natural resources of the Nation must be promptly developed and generously used to supply the people's needs, but we cannot safely allow them to be wasted, exploited, monopolized or controlled against the general good."
> —Theodore Roosevelt, "Platform of the Progressive Party" speech, August 7, 1912

of the measures that the club had accomplished with Roosevelt as its president was to encourage the protection of Yellowstone Park, which was achieved when the federal government passed the Park Protection Act in 1894.

Roosevelt occasionally had dreams of being president of the United States, but he had alienated many professional politicians with his efforts to abolish corruption. Because of this he believed that he wouldn't have the political support to win the U.S. presidency.

5

PRESIDENT ROOSEVELT

TEDDY ROOSEVELT FELT proud of his work as governor and enjoyed the position. He wrote to his sister Corinne, "Haven't we had fun being governor?" Later, he wrote, "On the whole, I have continued all my life to have a better time year after year."

In 1900, Roosevelt wanted a second term as governor. He had made it hard, though, for the big bosses and dishonest businessmen to continue their activities, so they opposed a second term. Senator Thomas Platt had powerful friends in big business who contributed to the Republican Party, and he was boss of the political machine. Platt figured that the best way to get

Senator Thomas Platt wanted to stop Roosevelt from interfering with the corrupt practices of Platt's friends, so Platt arranged for Roosevelt to become William McKinley's running mate in the 1900 presidential election. In this photo, McKinley's previous running mate, Garret Hobart, was replaced with Roosevelt. McKinley is seated on the left.

rid of Roosevelt was to arrange for him to be nominated for vice president of the United States.

Roosevelt was not entirely pleased. He believed that the office of vice president would not give him enough duties and he would not be as politically active as he wanted to be. Nevertheless, after friends and political associates encouraged him, Roosevelt allowed himself to be a candidate for nomination. The Republicans nominated him for vice president as William McKinley's running mate.

McKinley and Roosevelt won the election. The new president and vice president were inaugurated in 1901. Having started out dedicated to conservation issues, Teddy

Roosevelt never even considered being vice president. That wasn't all he hadn't planned on.

On September 14, 1901, President McKinley was shot and killed at the World's Fair in Buffalo, New York. Teddy Roosevelt became the 26th U.S. president, and at 42 years of age, the youngest man to ever hold that office. He was called the first modern president. Unfortunately for Senator Platt and the big bosses, Roosevelt set to work to restrain big business.

SQUARE DEAL

President Theodore Roosevelt strongly supported a better distribution of wealth. Even though he was from a privileged economic class, he wanted the federal government to defend the rights of all Americans and to provide for the poor. He supported measures to ensure the safety of foods and medicines by sponsoring the Pure Food and Drug Act. This political philosophy and the program that Roosevelt initiated were called the "Square Deal."

> *"We demand that big business give the people a square deal; in return we must insist that when any one engaged in big business honestly endeavors to do right he shall himself be given a square deal."*
>
> —Theodore Roosevelt, address before the Ohio Constitutional Convention, February 21, 1912

The United States had become an industrial nation. Businesses had grown, and big businesses were swallowing up smaller businesses. Roosevelt believed that the government needed to make sure that every American had a "square deal." One way Roosevelt attempted to achieve this was by breaking up big trusts.

TRUSTBUSTER

Small businesses often cannot compete with trusts, another name for big businesses. Roosevelt worked to break up the trusts that controlled the United States. The big bosses insinuated themselves into politics by bribing legislators, or lawmakers, to vote for laws that would enhance or solidify their businesses.

Roosevelt had more than 40 trusts brought to court to be broken up. Among these was the railroad conglomerate in the Northwest. After two years, Roosevelt was finally able to break up the railroad trust; for his efforts, Roosevelt was dubbed "Trustbuster."

AT HOME IN THE WHITE HOUSE

Edith Roosevelt wanted their home in the White House to be a place where the children would feel comfortable. She got rid of the heavy Victorian furniture and fancy trappings the house had when they moved in and redecorated in a simple style. Teddy made sure that he spent time with his children there. They took many walks and went on hikes along the Potomac. Teddy sometimes kept important dignitaries waiting while he finished playing with his children. Once, he abruptly left a meeting at four o'clock because he had promised his boys he would take them hunting. "I never keep boys waiting. It's a hard trial for a boy to wait," he told the members of the meeting.

The family lived at Sagamore Hill for three months during the summer. Whenever he could, Teddy joined the family there, where he played and romped with the children on the lawn, enjoyed boating, hiking, and skating, and played with the many unusual family pets. Most of the pets had names and all had distinct personalities. There were Skip, Pete, Jack, and Sailor Boy the dogs; Tom Quartz and Slippers the cats; Josiah the badger; Algonquin the pony; Eli Yale the macaw; Jonathan the piebald rat; Emily Spinach the garter snake; and many others. Teddy encouraged the children to have animals so that they would learn to be kind to beings that were weaker than themselves.

> "I don't think that any family has ever enjoyed the White House more than we have. . . . It is a wonderful privilege to have been here and to have been given the chance to do this work, and I should regard myself as having a small and mean mind if in the event of defeat, I felt soured at not having more instead of being thankful for having had so much."
>
> —Theodore Roosevelt, in a letter to his son, Kermit, regarding his reelection to the U.S. presidency

The fun wasn't confined to the outdoors. Never before or since had the White House been home to such a raucous, rambunctious bunch. Alice, the oldest, was a beautiful teen and seemed to do things just for their shock value. Against her parents' wishes, she smoked. She had a blue macaw and a pet garter snake, both of which she carried around and sometimes brought to White House functions. When a friend once asked Teddy why he didn't control his daughter, Teddy replied, "I can do one of two things. I can

Alice, Roosevelt's oldest daughter, was a beautiful young woman who often shocked the public with her outrageous behavior. She smoked and had unusual pets, including a garter snake she sometimes brought to formal White House events. "Alice Blue Gown," a popular song at the time, was written in her honor.

be president of the United States or I can control Sister [Alice]. I can't possibly do both."

The public loved Alice despite her antics. The popular song "Alice Blue Gown" was written for Alice, who often wore blue-gray dresses. In 1906, during her father's second term, Alice married Congressman Nicholas Longworth at a very glamorous and elaborate affair at the White House.

CONSERVATION GOALS

Roosevelt took trips to the wilderness during his presidency. In 1903, he went to Yosemite in California with naturalist John Muir. This journey further inspired him to do something to preserve the great gifts of nature.

Throughout his presidency, Roosevelt continued to develop a policy of conservation and to stress the importance of the involvement of the people to make it work. He believed that "the whole nation must undertake the task."

Roosevelt knew that the country's natural resources should be maintained and preserved because they would not last forever. This was a new concept to the people of the early 1900s; most believed that natural resources were inexhaustible. Roosevelt set out to educate his fellow countrymen about the fragility of the forests, waters, and animals. With his old friend and associate Gifford Pinchot, he developed a plan that addressed both water and forestry issues.

Irrigation

Since many people were likely to move to the western part of the country, Teddy saw a need for land that was arable, or able to be farmed for crops. Farms for crops and animals required ample water, so the dry lands of the West and the western Plains had to be irrigated to make it possible for people to farm it. Roosevelt proposed that water storage methods be used to store overflow waters from rivers and streams. The stored water could be used to irrigate the farmlands.

On June 17, 1902, Congress passed the Reclamation Act. Two dams were built that transformed arid desert into land suitable for farming: the Roosevelt Dam in Arizona and the Shoshone Dam in Wyoming.

Forestry and Wildlife

Up to this time, the Bureau of Forestry consisted of officials who knew nothing about and had never visited forestlands. Roosevelt urged Congress to appoint people trained in forestry to manage conservation issues. He also proposed protecting native plants and animals by setting up wildlife refuges. These refuges could be used as camping areas for people. Certain places were designated as "free camping grounds for the ever-increasing numbers of men and women who have learned to find rest, health, and recreation in the splendid forests and flower-clad meadows of the mountains." The refuges were very important in saving the bird population alone, since millions of birds had been killed for the millinery (hat) industry.

> *"A people without children would face a hopeless future. A country without trees is almost as hopeless."*
> —Theodore Roosevelt, "Letter to America's School Children," Arbor Day, 1907

ORIGIN OF THE TEDDY BEAR

Many of Roosevelt's friends were naturalists and environmentalists interested in the same things that he was. In 1903, Roosevelt visited Yellowstone National Park with naturalist John Burroughs. He later went camping in Yosemite in California with environmentalist John Muir. Nature always inspired Roosevelt to write, and he wrote well. He described his impression of Yosemite as follows:

> The first night [in Yosemite] was clear, and we lay down in the darkening aisle of the great Sequoia grove. The majestic trunks, beautiful in color and in symmetry, rose round us like the pillars of a mightier cathedral than ever was conceived even by the fervor of the Middle Ages.

In spite of his beliefs regarding the protection of wildlife, Teddy Roosevelt hunted game, including bears. He was often criticized for this. Perhaps this was an inconsistency in his character, but he believed that conservative hunting of game would still allow the animals to reproduce and to maintain their population.

Around this time, a story began to circulate that Roosevelt refused to shoot a small bear cub while on a hunting trip. It was a nice story but not exactly accurate. It was really an old, defenseless bear that he would not shoot. Still, American business ingenuity soon came forth with a stuffed baby bear named after the president: the Teddy Bear. The Teddy Bear celebrated its one hundredth anniversary in 2002 and is still one of the most popular toys among children of all ages.

CONSERVATION CONFERENCES

In May 1908, during his second term, President Roosevelt held a conference on conservation in Washington, D.C. Environmentalists, scientists, governors, congressmen, Supreme Court justices, and foreign representatives were invited. It was a great success, fueled by Roosevelt's enthusiasm and knowledge. The National Conservation Commission

PRESIDENT ROOSEVELT'S LEGACY

Conservationism

Theodore Roosevelt was a champion of conservation. In fact, an expandable conservation system was perhaps his most enduring legacy. With his experience in the West, he recognized the damage that floodwaters and intermittent drought can have on the land and on plant and animal life. Roosevelt's belief was that conservation means development as well as protection. Among his conservation measures were curbing the destruction of floods from the Mississippi River and its tributaries, protecting forestland trees from being overcut by lumbermen, developing methods of water storage and levees, and developing water power. With flood control and irrigation, deserts and swamps could be reclaimed to support millions of people. Roosevelt believed that we—meaning the federal government as well as all American citizens—have a moral obligation to pass on the land in a better condition to our children and all later descendants.

President Franklin Delano Roosevelt, Teddy's fifth cousin, set out to obtain relief for the unemployed and for those who were in danger of losing their farms and homes. A big part of doing this was establishing the Tennessee Valley Authority (TVA). The TVA is a federal corporation that operates the Wilson Dam and other dams as well as steam plants along the Tennessee River and its tributaries. The manifold purpose of the TVA is flood control, distribution of electricity, and the development of fertilizers. Control of floodwaters curbs soil erosions and loss of trees (deforestation).

Roosevelt is pictured with naturalist John Muir (standing front and right of Roosevelt) and several other men on a trip to Yosemite in 1903 in front of one of the huge redwood trees that populate the park. The trip further inspired Roosevelt's conservationist efforts.

was formed as a result of this meeting. The first task, to catalog all of the country's natural resources—an ambitious but worthwhile undertaking—was led by Gifford Pinchot.

The success of the 1908 conference inspired another conference in 1909. This one had more international attendees. From this meeting, a plan was set for an international convention to discuss the "identification, conservation, and managed use" of the natural resources of the world—a mammoth task.

OTHER GREAT ACCOMPLISHMENTS
The Panama Canal

Long before he was president, Roosevelt had encouraged joining the Atlantic and Pacific oceans with a canal, so that American ships could cross back and forth. In a sense, the building of this passageway would shrink the world. When Roosevelt took office, he made it happen. Congress passed the Spooner Bill, which authorized the construction of the Panama Canal, in June 1902.

The country of Panama, a colony of Colombia (then called New Granada), wanted the canal. Colombia agreed, but suddenly changed its mind. Furious, Panama started to revolt to obtain its independence. To keep Colombia from putting down the rebellion, the United States positioned an American gunboat in Panama's harbor. This resulted in Panama joyfully declaring its independence as a republic on November 6, 1903. President Roosevelt was criticized for his "gunboat diplomacy," but he retorted that he "lifted his foot and let it [the revolution] happen." This tactic is an example of Theodore Roosevelt's Big Stick Policy in foreign affairs—that is, to speak softly but carry a big stick.

> "There is a homely adage which runs, 'Speak softly and carry a big stick; you will go far.'"
>
> —Theodore Roosevelt, speech given at the Minnesota State Fair, September 2, 1901

Russo-Japanese War

By 1905, the Russians and the Japanese had been at war for about a year. Japan had a strong navy and crushed most of Russia's fleet. Roosevelt didn't think that a strong Japan (or a strong Russia) in the Pacific was in America's best interest. Both sides were tired of fighting, so Roosevelt persuaded representatives of each country to agree to a meeting in Portsmouth, New Hampshire, in the summer of 1905.

By September 5, after much haggling, both sides had compromised and signed a peace treaty. For his part in mediating the agreement, Teddy Roosevelt was awarded the Nobel Peace Prize, a prestigious award given to the person who has done the most or best work to promote brotherhood and peace among nations. He refused the $37,000 prize for himself, instead donating the money to a committee for industrial peace.

★　　　★　　　★

Fifty-one-year-old Theodore Roosevelt left the presidency in 1909, happy and still immensely popular after eight years in office. Unfortunately, Roosevelt's successor, William Howard Taft, did not have the same commitment to conservation and the other policies that Roosevelt had championed.

6

THE
LAST SAFARI

FREE FROM THE responsibilities of the presidency, Teddy went back to being a boy seeking adventure. In 1909, Teddy and son Kermit went on a 10-month safari to East Africa to hunt large game—rhinoceros, hippopotamus, elephants, lions, and cape buffalo. Kermit was a fitting companion for his father: He had finished school but did not yet have a career.

In many ways, Kermit was similar to Teddy. Kermit loved hunting, history, and languages. He read at least one book a day. He learned Spanish and French and taught himself Greek, Romany (Gypsy), and Sanskrit. He also wrote many books about hunting and exploration.

Teddy and his son Kermit went on an African safari in 1909. Roosevelt, pictured above with a rhinoceros that he killed on his trip, donated all of the animals he hunted to the Smithsonian in Washington, D.C., continuing his commitment to bringing wildlife and environmental issues to the public.

Andrew Carnegie financed the trip, and off they went with 60 books for Teddy to read and a staff of 260. Teddy had all the animals he killed stuffed and donated to the Smithsonian in Washington, D.C.

Teddy was disappointed that President Taft did not continue all of his policies. After the 10-month break from political life, Teddy was fueled to run for president again in 1912. The Republican Party didn't nominate him, but

the Progressive Party did, and he ran against Woodrow
Wilson and William Howard Taft.

When asked by a reporter about his health, Roosevelt
replied, "I feel fit as a bull moose." The symbol of the
Progressive Party then
became the bull moose,
and Teddy Roosevelt's
political struggle for the
presidency was called the
Bull Moose Campaign.

> *"This country belongs to the people who inhabit it. Its resources, its business, its institutions and its laws should be utilized, maintained or altered in whatever manner will best promote the general interest."*
>
> —Theodore Roosevelt, "Platform of the Progressive Party," August 7, 1912

When Roosevelt was
about to give a speech in
Milwaukee, Wisconsin, a
deranged man shot Roosevelt in the chest. Fortunately,
Roosevelt had his speech folded and tucked in his pocket,
which lessened the force of the bullet. Roosevelt took his
speech out of his pocket, which was torn from the bullet
and stained with his blood. Showing the papers to the
crowd, the unflappable Roosevelt said, "It takes more than
that to kill a Bull Moose," and began his speech. He was
later treated for the bullet wound at a local hospital.

In spite of his energetic campaigning, Roosevelt and
Taft lost to Woodrow Wilson in 1912. Roosevelt returned
to his home at Sagamore Hill and led a quiet life of
reading, writing, and listening to and identifying birds.

In 1917, 55-year-old Teddy Roosevelt and his son
Kermit went on another prolonged sponsored hunting
trip, this time to the jungles of Brazil. Asked why he would
take such a rigorous trip, Teddy said, "It is my last chance

to be a boy." Father and son set out on a trip down the one thousand-mile dangerous River of Doubt to the Amazon River. The pair met up with nightmarish perils of the tropical regions that they hadn't planned on: flesh-eating ants, vampire bats, poisonous snakes, and masses of biting insects. Teddy seriously injured his leg and then got malaria (a recurring infection from a mosquito bite that causes chills, fever, anemia, and an enlarged spleen) and dysentery (inflammation of the intestine causing spastic diarrhea and abdominal pain). He was lucky to get home alive. The river was later renamed Rio Teodoro (the River Theodore) in his honor.

After this trip, Roosevelt lost much of his vitality and energy.

The United States entered World War I in 1917. All of the Roosevelt sons served. On July 14, 1918, Teddy's youngest son, Quentin, an army pilot, was shot down and killed. This was a tremendous blow to Teddy; still, he was proud that his son died courageously in war. Serving one's country in wartime was a high personal priority for Teddy, if not the highest. He said:

> It is bitter that the young should die, but there are things worse than death; for nothing under heaven would I have had my sons act [by joining the armed forces] otherwise than as they acted.

In the fall of that year, Teddy Roosevelt was hospitalized for seven weeks. His strength never returned, and on

Theodore Roosevelt died on January 6, 1919 and was buried in Youngs Memorial Cemetery in Oyster Bay, New York. In a cable to his brothers, Archie announced their father's death, writing, "the old lion is dead."

January 6, 1919, he died in his sleep at Sagamore Hill at age 60. In a cable to his brothers, Archie announced their father's death: "The old lion is dead."

THE GREAT MASTER

A great president has a vision of an ideal country and works toward achieving that vision. President Theodore Roosevelt's vision for America was that of a fair and equal society (which is demonstrated by his Square Deal reform) living in a balanced and beautiful landscape (which he championed in his conservation efforts). The accomplishments of the first modern president, also known as the Conservation President, lay the foundation for the policies of future presidents and legislators.

No president since Teddy Roosevelt has been such a champion of the environment. He had long recognized that the country was using up its resources too quickly and worked to protect and maintain them. He created five national parks: Crater Lake in Oregon, Wind Cave in South Dakota, Platt Park in Oklahoma, Sully Hill in North Dakota, and Mesa Verdi in Colorado. He established 18 national landmarks, such as Muir Woods and the Grand Canyon. He created 512 bird sanctuaries, 4 big game refuges, and a national game reserve (the first of its kind). He added 43 million acres to the national forests. Teddy Roosevelt also wrote 30 books that reflected his love and knowledge of birds and of all nature. He was able to identify the sounds of almost every songbird in North America.

> *"Far better is it to dare mighty things, to win glorious triumphs even though checkered by failure, than to rank with those poor spirits who neither enjoy much nor suffer much because they live in a gray twilight that knows neither victory nor defeat."*
> —Theodore Roosevelt

As a trustbuster, he broke up big business and paved the way for fair labor practices. He believed that everyone must work. As a reformer, he publicly attacked corruption.

As the 26th president of the United States and the first "modern" president, Roosevelt and his vision of a strong and vibrant United States led the country into the twentieth century. With his powerful personality and determination, Roosevelt worked tirelessly toward achieving America's democratic ideals.

He was an original thinker, and his role in the construction of the Panama Canal effectively made the world smaller. He also had strong foreign policies. He worked toward making peace and ended the war between Russia and Japan, for which he received the Nobel Peace Prize. On January 16, 2001, Teddy Roosevelt was posthumously awarded the Congressional Medal of Honor for his valor during the Spanish-American War.

Described as an orator, statesman, historian, cowboy, explorer, hunter, naturalist, humanitarian, and philanthropist, Teddy Roosevelt's great energy and dynamic personality made him stand out as a character bigger than life. These unique personal traits, along with his vigorous government reform efforts and strong foreign policy, created a legend that persists today. In the United States, the spirit of Teddy Roosevelt is still very much alive: The country's beautiful national parks, enterprising attitude, and belief in the importance of the common man are all testaments to his enduring legacy. Most importantly, he emerged through history as one of the strongest and most influential presidents. His safari guides in Africa called him Buana Makuha, "great master."

THE PRESIDENTS
OF THE
UNITED STATES

George Washington
1789–1797

John Adams
1797–1801

Thomas Jefferson
1801–1809

James Madison
1809–1817

James Monroe
1817–1825

John Quincy Adams
1825–1829

Andrew Jackson
1829–1837

Martin Van Buren
1837–1841

William Henry
Harrison
1841

John Tyler
1841–1845

James Polk
1845–1849

Zachary Taylor
1849–1850

Millard Filmore
1850–1853

Franklin Pierce
1853–1857

James Buchanan
1857–1861

Abraham Lincoln
1861–1865

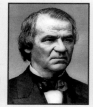

Andrew Johnson
1865–1869

Ulysses S. Grant
1869–1877

Rutherford B. Hayes
1877–1881

James Garfield
1881

Chester Arthur
1881–1885

Grover Cleveland
1885–1889

Benjamin Harrison
1889–1893

Grover Cleveland
1893-1897

William McKinley
1897–1901

Theodore Roosevelt
1901–1909

William H. Taft
1909–1913

Woodrow Wilson
1913–1921

Warren Harding
1921–1923

Calvin Coolidge
1923–1929

Herbert Hoover
1929–1933

Franklin D. Roo-
sevelt 1933–1945

Harry S. Truman
1945–1953

Dwight Eisenhower
1953–1961

John F. Kennedy
1961–1963

Lyndon Johnson
1963–1969

Richard Nixon
1969–1974

Gerald Ford
1974–1977

Jimmy Carter
1977–1981

Ronald Reagan
1981–1989

George H.W. Bush
1989–1993

William J. Clinton
1993–2001

George W. Bush
2001–

Note: Dates indicate years of
presidential service.
Source: www.whitehouse.gov

Presidential Fact File

THE CONSTITUTION

Article II of the Constitution of the United States outlines several requirements for the president of the United States, including:

- ★ **Age:** The president must be at least 35 years old.
- ★ **Citizenship:** The president must be a U.S. citizen.
- ★ **Residency:** The president must have lived in the United States for at least 14 years.
- ★ **Oath of Office:** On his inauguration, the president takes this oath: "I do solemnly swear (or affirm) that I will faithfully execute the office of President of the United States, and will to the best of my ability, preserve, protect and defend the Constitution of the United States."
- ★ **Term:** A presidential term lasts four years.

PRESIDENTIAL POWERS

The president has many distinct powers as outlined in and interpreted from the Constitution. The president:

- ★ Submits many proposals to Congress for regulatory, social, and economic reforms.
- ★ Appoints federal judges with the Senate's approval.
- ★ Prepares treaties with foreign nations to be approved by the Senate.
- ★ Can veto laws passed by Congress.
- ★ Acts as commander in chief of the military to oversee military strategy and actions.
- ★ Appoints members of the Cabinet and many other agencies and administrations with the Senate's approval.
- ★ Can declare martial law (control of local governments within the country) in times of national crisis.

PRESIDENTIAL FACT FILE

TRADITION

Many parts of the presidency developed out of tradition. The traditions listed below are but a few that are associated with the U.S. presidency.

★ After taking his oath of office, George Washington added, "So help me God." Numerous presidents since Washington have also added this phrase to their oath.

★ Originally, the Constitution limited the term of the presidency to four years, but did not limit the number of terms a president could serve. Presidents, following the precedent set by George Washington, traditionally served only two terms. After Franklin Roosevelt was elected to four terms, however, Congress amended the Constitution to restrict presidents to only two.

★ James Monroe was the first president to have his inauguration outside the Capitol. From his inauguration in 1817 to Jimmy Carter's inauguration in 1977, it was held on the Capitol's east portico. Ronald Reagan broke from this tradition in 1981 when he was inaugurated on the west portico to face his home state, California. Since 1981, all presidential inaugurations have been held on the west portico of the Capitol.

★ Not all presidential traditions are serious, however. One of the more fun activities connected with the presidency began when President William Howard Taft ceremoniously threw out the first pitch of the new baseball season in 1910.  Presidents since Taft have carried on this tradition, including Woodrow Wilson, who is pictured here as he throws the first pitch of the 1916 season. In more recent years, the president has also opened the All-Star and World Series games.

PRESIDENTIAL FACT FILE

THE WHITE HOUSE

Although George Washington was involved with the planning of the White House, he never lived there. It has been, however, the official residence of every president beginning with John Adams, the second U.S. president. The  building was completed approximately in 1800, although it has undergone several renovations since then. It was the first public building constructed in Washington, D.C. The White House has 132 rooms, several of which are open to the public. Private rooms include those for administration and the president's personal residence. For an online tour of the White House and other interesting facts, visit the official White House website, *http://www.whitehouse.gov*.

THE PRESIDENTIAL SEAL

A committee began planning the presidential seal in 1777. It was completed in 1782. The seal appears as an official stamp on medals, stationery, and documents, among other items. Originally, the eagle faced right toward the  arrows (a symbol of war) that it held in its talons. In 1945, President Truman had the seal altered so that the eagle's head instead faced left toward the olive branch (a symbol of peace), because he believed the president should be prepared for war but always look toward peace.

PRESIDENT THEODORE ROOSEVELT IN PROFILE

PERSONAL

Name: Theodore Roosevelt

Birth date: October 27, 1858

Birth place: New York, New York

Father: Theodore Roosevelt

Mother: Martha Bulloch

Wife: Alice Hathaway Lee (d. 1884); Edith Kermit Carow

Children: Alice (with Lee); Ted, Kermit, Ethel, Archie, and Quentin (with Carow)

Death date: January 6, 1919

Death place: Oyster Bay, New York

POLITICAL

Years in office: 1901–1909

Vice president: Charles Warren Fairbanks

Occupations before presidency: Author, New York State assemblyman, U.S. civil service commissioner, assistant secretary of the U.S. Navy, New York governor, New York City police commissioner, vice president to President William McKinley

Political party: Republican (later Progressive)

Major achievements of presidency: Square Deal principles, the Panama Canal, National Conservation Commission, "trust busting," government reform

Nicknames: Trustbuster, Teddy, the Conservation President

Presidential library: The Theodore Roosevelt Collection at
Harvard's Houghton Library
Harvard University
Cambridge, MA 02138
617-384-7938
http://www.theodoreroosevelt.org/modern/harvardcol.htm

Tributes:

Mount Rushmore
(Keystone, S.D.; *http://www.nps.gov/moru/*);

Theodore Roosevelt National Park
(Medora, N.D.; *http://www.nps.gov/thro/*);

Sagamore Hill
(Oyster Bay, N.Y.; *http://www.nps.gov/sahi/*)

1858	Theodore Roosevelt Jr. is born on October 27 in New York City, the second child of Theodore Roosevelt and Martha Bulloch Roosevelt.
1861–1865	The Civil War divides the United States.
1866	Theodore opens the Roosevelt Museum of Natural History in his room.
1876	Theodore enters Harvard College in Boston.
1880	Teddy graduates from Harvard and marries Alice Hathaway Lee.
1881–1882	Teddy attends Columbia Law School, has a belated European honeymoon with Alice, and climbs the Matterhorn.
1882–1884	Teddy serves three terms as a New York State assemblyman in Albany.
1884	Baby Alice is born, Alice Lee Roosevelt dies, and Mittie Roosevelt dies. Teddy goes to the Dakota Territory.
1885	Teddy becomes engaged to Edith Carow.
1886	Teddy runs for mayor of New York City and is defeated. He marries Edith.
1889–1895	Teddy becomes the United States civil service commissioner.
1895–1896	Teddy is appointed New York City police commissioner.
1897	Teddy and Edith's sixth and last child Quentin born.
1897–1898	Roosevelt becomes assistant secretary of the U.S. Navy.
1898	The Spanish-American War begins; Roosevelt resigns from the navy, forms the Rough Riders, and fights in Cuba.

CHRONOLOGY

1898   Roosevelt is elected governor of New York at age 39.

1901

March   Roosevelt becomes vice president of the United States.

September   President William McKinley is shot and killed in Buffalo, New York. Teddy Roosevelt is sworn in as 26th president at age 42.

1901–1909   Roosevelt finishes his first term as president and is elected for another.

1902   Work on the Panama Canal is begins.

1905   Roosevelt mediates the end to the Russo-Japanese War and receives Nobel Peace Prize for his efforts.

1906   Alice marries Congressman Nicholas Longworth at the White House.

1910   Teddy goes on an African safari with Kermit.

1912   The Progressive Party backs Roosevelt's unsuccessful Bull Moose Campaign for the presidency.

1914   Teddy goes on a safari to Brazil with Kermit to map the unexplored River of Doubt. He suffers a severe leg injury, malaria, and dysentery. The first ship passes through completed Panama Canal.

1914–1918   World War I rages in Europe; all four Roosevelt sons serve.

1919   Theodore Roosevelt dies in his sleep at Sagamore Hill.

BIBLIOGRAPHY

Auchincloss, Louis. *Theodore Roosevelt.* New York: Henry Holt and Company, 2001.

Burns, James MacGregor, and Susan Dunn. *The Three Roosevelts.* New York: Atlantic Monthly Press, 2001.

DeStefano, Susan. *Theodore Roosevelt: Conservation President.* Breckenridge, Colo.: Twenty-First Century Books, 1993.

Edey, Maitland, ed. *This Fabulous Century: 1900–1910.* New York: Time-Life Books, 1969.

Fritz, Jean. *Bully for You, Teddy Roosevelt.* New York: G.P. Putnam's Sons Books for Young Readers, 1991.

Kerr, Joan Paterson. *A Bully Father: Theodore Roosevelt's Letters to His Children.* New York: Random House, 1995.

McCullough, David. *Mornings on Horseback.* New York: Simon and Schuster, 1981.

Quackenbush, Robert. *Don't You Dare Shoot That Bear!* Upper Saddle River, N.J.: Prentice Hall, 1984.

Morgan, Ted. *FDR.* New York: Simon and Schuster, 1985.

Morris, Edmund. *Theodore Rex.* New York: Random House, 2001.

Renehan, Edward J., Jr. *The Lions' Pride: Theodore Roosevelt and His Family in Peace and War.* New York: Oxford University Press, 1998.

BIBLIOGRAPHY

WEBSITES

The Theodore Roosevelt Collection at Bartleby.com
http://www.bartleby.com/people/RsvltT.html

The American Experience: The Presidents
http://www.pbs.org/amex/presidents

Theodore Roosevelt Association
http://www.theodoreroosevelt.org

U.S. Diplomatic Mission to Germany: Famous Speeches
http://www.usembassy.de/usa/etexts/speeches/

The White House: Biography of Theodore Roosevelt
http://www.whitehouse.gov/history/presidents/tr26.html

FURTHER READING

Donn, Linda. *The Roosevelt Cousins.* New York: Alfred Knopf, 2001.

Gaines, Ann Graham. *Theodore Roosevelt.* Chanhassen, Minn.: The Child's World, Inc., 2002.

Lawson, Don. *The United States in the Spanish-American War.* New York: Abelard-Schuman, 1976.

Mothner, Ira. *Man of Action.* New York: Platt & Munk, 1966.

Roosevelt, Theodore. *The Rough Riders.* Dallas: Taylor Publishing, 1997.

Whitelaw, Nancy. *Theodore Roosevelt Takes Charge.* Morton Grove, Ill.: Albert Whitman and Company, 1992.

WEBSITES

The American President
http://www.americanpresident.org

Presidential Museums.com
http://www.presidentialmuseums.com

Theodore Roosevelt National Park
http://www.nps.gov/thro/

Theodore Roosevelt: His Life and Times on Film
http://memory.loc.gov/ammem/trfhtml/trfhome.html

Theodore Roosevelt Papers at the Library of Congress
http://memory.loc.gov/ammem/trhtml/trhome.html

The Internet Public Library: Theodore Roosevelt
http://ipl.si.umich.edu/div/potus/troosevelt.html

Theodore Roosevelt: Icon of the American Century
http://www.npg.si.edu/exh/roosevelt/

The American Experience: Theodore Roosevelt
http://www.pbs.org/wgbh/amex/tr/

The Nobel e-Museum: Theodore Roosevelt
http://www.nobel.se/peace/laureates/1906/roosevelt-bio.html

Meet Amazing Americans: Theodore Roosevelt
http://www.americaslibrary.gov/cgi-bin/page.cgi/aa/roosevelt

INDEX

Africa, Roosevelt's safari
in, 20, 74-75, 81
Alabama, and Civil War,
14-15
Alger, Russell A., 55
"Alice Blue Gown,"
as song for Alice
Roosevelt, 65
Amazon River, Roosevelt's
safari to, 77
American Indians, and
buffalo, 42
Art Club, Roosevelt
involved in at Harvard,
26
Associated Press, and
Roosevelt's letter getting
army home from Cuba,
55-56
Asthma, Roosevelt suffer-
ing from
in childhood, 15
and hunting for buffalo,
32
and improvement in
college years, 26
and treatment in health
spa, 31-32

Big business, Roosevelt's
fight against as presi-
dent, 62-63, 79
Big Stick Policy, 72
Birds, Roosevelt's interest
in, 16
and collecting speci-
mens, 20, 21
and establishing sanctu-
aries, 67, 79
in retirement at
Sagamore Hill, 79
and writing books, 79
Blaine, James G., 33
Boone and Crockett Club,
42, 59
Boone, Daniel, Roosevelt's
mother's stories about,
14

Brazil, Roosevelt's safari
in, 76-77
Bright's disease, Roosevelt's
first wife dying from,
32, 33
Bronco busting, Roosevelt
participating in, 36
Buffalo. *See* Dakota
Territory, Roosevelt's
interest in buffalo in
Buffalo Bill, 10
Bull Moose Campaign,
75-76
Bulloch, Daniel (uncle),
14-15
Bulloch, Irvine (uncle),
15
Bulloch, James (uncle),
14
Bureau of Forestry, 67
Burroughs, John, 68

Carnegie, Andrew, 75
Catskill Mountains,
Roosevelt at spa in,
31-32
Chandler, William, 50
Children's Aid Society,
Roosevelt's father
establishing, 13
Civil War
Roosevelt's father's
support for, 15, 56
Roosevelt's mother's
family in, 14-15
substitutes paid to
fight in, 15
Columbia University,
Roosevelt attending law
school at, 29, 30
Congressional Medal
of Honor
Roosevelt awarded,
80
Roosevelt desiring,
56
Conservation, Roosevelt's
interest in, 37, 42

and conferences, 69,
71
See also National
history/environment,
Roosevelt's interest in
Corruption, Roosevelt's
fight against, 79
as assemblyman in
New York State
legislature, 31
as governor of New
York State, 58, 59
as New York City
police commissioner,
45-47
as U.S. civil service
commissioner, 44
as vice president, 60-
62
as young member of
New York City
Republican Party, 30
Cowboy, Roosevelt as,
34-37
Crater Lake National
Park, 79
Crockett, Davy, Roosevelt's
mother's stories about,
14
Cuba, and Spanish-
American War, 48, 50-
56, 58, 80

Dakota Territory,
Roosevelt's interest in
buffalo in
and American Indians,
42
as cattle rancher, 34-37,
38, 40
and Elkhorn Ranch, 35,
38, 40, 41, 44
and environmental
concerns, 37, 42
and hunting for buffalo,
32
and investing in herd,
32, 35

Index

INDEX

PICTURE CREDITS

ACKNOWLEDGMENTS

Thank you to Celebrity Speakers Intl. for coordinating Mr. Cronkite's contribution to this book.

ABOUT THE CONTRIBUTORS

Alison Turnbull Kelley holds a B.A. in Classical Languages from Chestnut Hill College. She is working toward her Ph.D. in holistic nutrition. A freelance writer and editor of medical textbooks and articles for many years, she has also published articles and a play for young people. She lives in Newtown, Bucks County, Pennsylvania.

Walter Cronkite has covered virtually every major news event during his more than 60 years in journalism, during which he earned a reputation for being "the most trusted man in America." He began his career as a reporter for the United Press during World War II, taking part in the beachhead assaults of Normandy and covering the Nuremberg trials. He then joined *CBS News* in Washington, D.C., where he was the news anchor for political convention and election coverage from 1952 to 1980. CBS debuted its first half-hour weeknight news program with Mr. Cronkite's interview of President John F. Kennedy in 1963. Mr. Cronkite was inducted into the Academy of Television Arts and Sciences in 1985 and has written several books. He lives in New York City with his wife of 59 years.